W9-ABX-447

Better Homes and Gardens®

LAWNS GROUND COVERS AND VINES

Excerpted from Better Homes and Gardens® *STEP-BY-STEP SUCCESSFUL GARDENING*

© Copyright 1988 by Meredith Corporation, Des Moines, Iowa.
All Rights Reserved. Printed in the United States of America.
First Edition. First Printing.
ISBN: 0-696-01807-1

BETTER HOMES AND GARDENS® BOOKS

Editor: Gerald M. Knox
Art Director: Ernest Shelton
Managing Editor: David A. Kirchner
Editorial Project Managers: James D. Blume, Marsha Jahns,
  Rosanne Weber Mattson, Mary Helen Schiltz

Garden, Projects, and New Products Editor:
  Douglas A. Jimerson
Associate Editor: Jane Austin McKeon

Associate Art Directors: Linda Ford Vermie,
  Neoma Thomas, Randall Yontz
Assistant Art Directors: Lynda Haupert, Harijs Priekulis,
  Tom Wegner
Graphic Designers: Mary Schlueter Bendgen, Mike Burns,
  Brian Wignall
Art Production: Director: John Berg;
  Associate: Joe Heuer
  Office Manager: Michaela Lester

President, Book Group: Fred Stines
Vice President, General Manager: Jeramy Lanigan
Vice President, Retail Marketing: Jamie L. Martin
Vice President, Administrative Services: Rick Rundall

BETTER HOMES AND GARDENS® MAGAZINE
President, Magazine Group: James A. Autry
Vice President, Editorial Director: Doris Eby
Executive Director, Editorial Services: Duane L. Gregg

LAWNS, GROUND COVERS, AND VINES
Editorial Project Manager: Rosanne Weber Mattson
Graphic Designer: Brian Wignall
Electronic Text Processor: Paula Forest

CONTENTS

SOIL

Every gardener wishes for large and healthy plants, big, bright flowers, luscious, record-breaking vegetables, and juicy, mouth-watering fruits. Such blue-ribbon gardening results require some commonsense techniques; more important, they depend on one basic ingredient: good soil. By starting from the ground up, you can help provide the essentials to give plant roots space, water, food, oxygen, and minerals for ideal growing conditions.

TYPES OF SOIL

■ In order to know how to treat your soil properly so it will do its best for you, you need to know a little about its texture. Soil consists of three types of particles: sand, the largest; clay, the smallest; and silt, which falls in between. The ideal soil—loam—balances all three types.

Sandy soils dry out quickly and leach fertilizer rapidly, but these soils drain well. Clay soils are heavy, hold excessive water, and have poor aeration, yet hold on to fertilizer well. Soil that is heavy with clay will stick to your shovel; when the soil is moist, you can squeeze it with your fingers into a tight ball.

SOIL IMPROVEMENTS

■ You'll rarely find ideal soil in your garden, but you can improve what you find to achieve healthier plant growth and better produce. The secret to soil improvement lies in organic matter, in the form of peat moss, leaf mold, manure, or compost. You should work in enough organic matter to make it about 25 percent of your finished soil.

If possible, add organic matter in the fall to give the microorganisms in the soil plenty of time to decompose the material before spring planting. After working in organic matter, add any other amendments, such as bonemeal or superphosphate for good root growth. Spade or till soil to a depth of 12 to 24 inches, breaking large chunks into smaller particles. You can also improve soil with double digging, which switches richer topsoil to the root zone.

UNDERSTANDING pH

■ The term pH measures how the soil fits on the acidic-basic scale, indicated by a number between 0 and 14. The

number 7 is neutral, with 0 being most acidic and 14 most basic. The pH is important because nutrient availability, soil organisms, and solubility of toxins depend on it. Although some plants like a low pH, most prefer a pH between 6 and 7. A pH that is too low should be raised with ground dolomitic limestone; one that is too high can be lowered with sulfur. Gypsum will condition soil without affecting pH.

Because you can't tell what's in soil by looking at it, it's a good idea to have your soil tested every few years. A simple test will indicate pH. Other tests can be run for organic matter and nutrients. Collect the soil from several areas, being careful not to include mulch, thatch, or roots. Mix the soils together in a quart jar. Labs, county agents, and some garden centers test soil, or you can do it yourself with a purchased kit.

WATER

Mother Nature provides us with water in the form of rain, dew, and underground sources. Sometimes, however, these natural sources aren't enough. Extreme heat and wind, for example, make soil moisture evaporate very quickly. When temperatures soar or winds increase, plants will lose greater amounts of water through their leaves, and you'll need to replenish the water more often.

HOW MUCH, HOW OFTEN

■ Gardeners often ask the question, "How often should I water, and how much should I apply?" There isn't a simple answer. Soil texture is a key factor; clay soils can hold three times as much water as sandy soils, and will not need to be watered as frequently. Improving your soil as described on pages 4 and 5 will allow the soil to use and conserve water most efficiently.

As a rule of thumb, apply one inch of water per watering, and don't water again until the soil surface dries. The time it takes to apply one inch of water depends on your method of watering and your water pressure. A simple and

inexpensive way to find your watering time is to set out a rain gauge or several empty cans, and time how long it takes to collect an inch of water, using your watering method.

WATERING TECHNIQUES

■ For best results, water to soak the soil deeply. Light and frequent waterings use more water and encourage shallow roots, making your plants more vulnerable to damage from drought, weeds, and diseases. Deep waterings lead to desirable long roots.

To prevent sacrificing moisture to evaporation, avoid watering on a windy day. If your garden is in an exposed location, install a hedge or windbreak to temper the wind's force. Remember also that because large trees rob water from smaller shrubs nearby, you may need to apply extra water. Street-side trees, surrounded by pavement, often do not receive enough water. You can help by digging a well, which will collect water, around the trunk.

WATERING METHODS

■ The system you choose to water your garden depends on your property, preference, and budget. If you use oscillat-

ing or rotating sprinklers, be sure that the watered areas overlap. Water during cool morning hours, when less moisture will dissipate. Early watering also lets foliage dry before evening, which prevents fungus diseases.

A sprinkler needs a garden hose to get the job done. Hoses come in a variety of sizes: the ½-inch hose is lightweight; the ⅝-inch hose is the most common size; and the ¾-inch hose is for heavy-duty work. To prevent kinks, store all hoses rolled up. Empty hoses in the fall before storing for the winter.

Watering by hand is time-consuming and inefficient for large areas, but necessary for container plants, new seedlings, and hanging baskets.

A newer system, referred to as drip irrigation, has recently become popular. In this system, water travels to the plants through tiny holes in a hose laid on the ground, or by small extenders from the main hose. Drip irrigation takes longer, but uses 30 percent less water and produces better growth.

MULCHING

■ To conserve moisture in the soil and cut down on the amount of supplementary water needed, lay a 2- to 3-inch

layer of mulch on the ground surrounding plants. A mulch will also keep down weeds (which compete for soil moisture), and looks attractive. Recommended mulches include shredded bark, grass clippings, straw, pine needles, leaf mold, bean hulls, or a layer of black plastic. Organic mulches have the added benefit of enriching the soil as they decompose.

FERTILIZER

Plants are like the people that care for them. They are born, they grow, they reproduce, and they die. During this process they need light, water, food, air, and the right temperature to survive and thrive. We can't always control all of the elements in our plants' environment, but we can be certain that they receive the right nutrition. Knowing their fertilizer needs is important.

THE ELEMENTS

■ Good plant growth requires 16 basic elements. If any of these elements are missing or not present in the correct amounts, plants will grow poorly, and produce fewer and smaller flowers and fruits. The necessary elements include carbon, hydrogen, nitrogen, phosphorus, potassium, calcium, magnesium, sulfur, and minor elements such as manganese, copper, zinc, molybdenum, chlorine, boron, and iron.

Water and air provide plants with carbon, hydrogen, and nitrogen. Many other elements also naturally abound and are not a matter for concern. Nitrogen, phosphorus, and potassium form a "complete" fertilizer and need to be regularly added to soil.

Nitrogen (N) is found in every plant cell as a part of many proteins and of chlorophyll. It encourages vegetative growth and contributes to a dark green color. Phosphorus (P) stimulates root growth and is vital to photosynthesis. It plays a key role in flowering and fruiting. Potassium (K) has a role in metabolism, contributes to hardiness and disease resistance, and affects respiration and transpiration.

Calcium is needed for new growth. If it isn't adequately present in your soil, you can apply it through lime or gypsum. Dolomitic limestone, the best, also contains magnesium, needed for enzyme action and for moving phosphorus through the plant. Sulfur, an important component of plant protein, is available from air, water, organic matter, or application. Trace (or minor) elements, so named because they are needed in small doses, play a role in photosynthesis, enzyme action, overall plant growth, and nutrient absorption. All complete fertilizers contain N, P, and K and often other elements.

ORGANIC VS. INORGANIC

■ Fertilizers are classed as organic or inorganic. True organic fertilizers come from animal and plant wastes. Examples are blood meal, manures, and cottonseed meal. Organic fertilizers are slow-acting and nonburning, but are bulky, often low in nitrogen, and unpredictable in their nutrient release.

Inorganic fertilizers are chemicals such as potassium, ammonium nitrates, and ammonium phosphates. They are very water soluble, but can burn and leach quickly. If you apply inorganic fertilizers in concentrated amounts, keep them from direct contact with roots and foliage to avoid killing the plants instead of nurturing them.

A group of fertilizers called synthetic organics—such as urea, ureaformaldehyde, and IBDU—release nutrients slowly, based on water or soil temperature. They burn and leach less.

On fertilizer labels, you'll see numbers such as 10-6-4, 5-10-5, or 20-20-20, which stand for the percentages of N, P, and K in that order. Use a high N for lawns, a high P for flowering or fruiting plants, or a balance for foliage. You'll also see the term WIN, which stands for Water Insoluble Nitrogen. A WIN of less than 15 percent means a fast-acting fertilizer, and one over 30 percent releases slowly.

HOW TO APPLY

■ Apply granular fertilizers to soil by hand or with a spreader, and work them into the top two or three inches of soil, being careful not to damage shallow roots. Apply fertilizers evenly over the root area; avoid applying fertilizer to the stem or crown of plants. Liquid fertilizers should be applied to the soil or foliage. To avoid burning plants, water well beforehand and do not apply too much fertilizer.

Large trees and shrubs can be fed by driving plant spikes into the ground or by injecting fertilizer with a root feeder. Because the majority of a tree's feeder roots—the ones that can use nutrients—lie in the top 10 to 12 inches of soil, feeding too deeply will not help get the nutrients to the right place.

WHEN TO APPLY

■ Fertilize plants when growth is at its peak or when they're producing flowers or fruits. Don't encourage late summer growth, because it can be harmed by oncoming cold weather. One popular method is late-fall dormant feeding. With this method, fertilizer is applied after plants stop growing, and remains in the soil over winter so it can be used when root growth starts in early spring.

TOOLS

Choose the right tool for the job. That sage advice is as true in the garden as it is in the workshop indoors. A high-quality tool will last longer; it also will make gardening easier and more enjoyable. Most tools come in a variety of styles and sizes. They may have short or long handles, and round or square surfaces. At the store, try the tools out for grip and reach before you buy.

SPADES AND SHOVELS

■ A spade is a kind of shovel. There are many types of spades to choose from. Use rounded, pointed, or straight, flat blades for digging and mixing soil, or working in organic matter and fertilizer. A shovel has a rounder blade and works best for lifting and moving soil or other materials.

When using a spade, push it down into the soil with your foot, push back on the handle, and roll soil to the side. Keep the blade clean, free of rust, and oiled. Tap out nicks with a hammer.

TROWELS

■ Trowels are hand tools for planting annuals, perennials, bulbs, and other small plants. Long, narrow trowels work best for digging holes in tight places. Invest in a good trowel, because the shaft can bend easily on inexpensive types. As with shovels, keep trowels clean and oiled.

HOES

■ Hoes break up soil and remove weeds, a technique called cultivation. Hoes can be flat across or have curved fingers. To use a hoe, pull the cutting edge toward you, taking up weeds at the same time. Keep your hoe sharp by using a file or a grinding wheel. Dull hoes bend weeds but don't cut them.

RAKES

■ Rakes have a multitude of uses, from smoothing soil and seedbeds to removing leaves and other debris from lawns. Leaf and grass rakes are usually made of bamboo or metal. Large rakes will help you get leaves cleaned up quickly in the fall; small rakes (or rakes that are adjustable) will help you get into those hard-to-reach spots under bushes or in window wells.

SPADING FORKS

■ When digging perennials, tubers, or bulbs for dividing, use a spading fork. It helps loosen the soil around the roots without damaging them. Because the tines will break up clumps more easily than a spade will, this tool also comes in handy for digging through very heavy garden soil.

TOOLS FOR PRUNING

■ Standard pruning shears can be either the blade-and-anvil type or hook-and-blade type, and are used for cutting trees, shrubs, or stems up to about the thickness of a pencil. Make larger cuts with loppers, which have long handles for added leverage. Look for pruning saws and pole pruners to use on thick

and hard-to-reach branches. For very large branches or big pruning jobs, consider either a hand or power chain saw to make the task easier.

For shaping hedges, choose one of the many hedge clippers available. If you're short—or your hedges are tall—try clippers with extra-long handles. For trimming areas where the lawn mower won't reach, use special grass shears or string weeders and trimmers; don't use them for tougher jobs because they may break easily.

LAWN MOWERS
■ Walk-behind mowers are best suited for lawn care on small lots-or on yards with a profusion of trees, fences, or other solid obstacles. Consider an electric mower if your yard is less than 10,000 square feet. (Cord length will reach this area.) For large, unobstructed lawns, you'll save time and energy if you make an extra investment in a riding mower or a self-propelled, walk-behind type.

LAWNS IN THE LANDSCAPE

A beautiful lawn begins with careful planning. The type of grass you plant will depend largely upon your landscape design and how you plan to use the lawned area. Formal flower borders should be set off by a complementary, fine-textured turf that is kept edged and closely manicured. A durable, coarser turf is more appropriate for an area that gets a lot of traffic or is used by children for play. An informal setting doesn't require meticulous upkeep.

SEED VS. SOD
■ Starting from seed is the most economical way to grow a lawn, but this method requires attention to planning, preparing, planting, and watering. If you have an area where seeding is difficult, such as a slope, or you want a lawn in a hurry (and are willing to spend more money), sodding is the route to follow. Some of the warm-season grasses should be started with stems or sod.

CHOOSING THE RIGHT MIX
■ Your climate is a big factor in what grasses you choose. Grasses are generally described as cool-season for the northern part of the country, and warm-season for southern areas. Cool-season grasses grow best in spring and fall; warm-season types grow fastest in summer and are not as winter-hardy.

Mixtures of several grass types work best for most lawns. That way, even if disease strikes, the damage probably will be limited to just one of the grasses in the mixture. By mixing a spring performer with a drought-tolerant summer grower, you'll help your lawn look good all year. To be sure of success when seeding a new lawn, choose a high-quality seed mixture containing very little "crop" or weed seeds. Bargain brands may germinate poorly.

COOL-SEASON GRASSES
■ Among the best cool-season types are: *Kentucky bluegrass*—One of the most popular. It requires moderate care to grow dense, dark, and medium-textured. *Fescue*—Usually combined with bluegrasses, it tolerates shade and dry conditions, and seldom needs fertilizing. *Tall fescue*—Relatively new in popularity, this grass is drought-tolerant and excellent for high-traffic areas. *Perennial ryegrass*—Quick growing and tough. It makes a fine-textured lawn when mixed with Kentucky bluegrass. *Bent grass*—Needs frequent watering and fertilizing. Best used for a golf course.

WARM-SEASON GRASSES
■ Recommended warm-season grasses are: *Bermuda grass*—Most drought-tolerant. Its excellent wearability makes it a good choice for play areas. *St. Augustine*—Good for shade. This is a coarse, nondurable grass. *Zoysia*—Heat- and drought-resistant, but late to turn green in the spring. Sometimes used in northern lawns for its toughness.

MOWING TECHNIQUES
■ You'll need to mow your lawn regularly to keep it looking its best. Cutting height depends on the type of grass and the time of year. Mow often enough so that not more than one-third is cut off at one time. In shady spots, cut grass less frequently and at a height of ½ inch taller than normal. Keep the blades of your lawn mower sharpened to avoid damaging grass tips.

STARTING A LAWN

The best time to start a new lawn is in the spring or early fall, when days are cool and moist and weeds are less of a threat. Seeding in early fall often provides the best results because it gives the lawn time to become well established before heavy frosts hit.

The first step in starting a lawn from scratch is to properly prepare the soil. (See opposite page.) To be sure of your soil conditions, have your soil tested for fertility and pH. Adequate levels of phosphorus and potassium are important for vigorous root growth, so you'll want to add these nutrients if the soil test shows they're needed. The ideal pH for lawns is between 6.0 and 7.0. If you need to raise the pH, use dolomitic limestone at the rate of 50 pounds per 1,000 square feet. If you need to lower it, use powdered sulfur.

Broadcast seeds with a mechanical spreader at the rate recommended on the seed package; overseeding will cause the tiny grass plants to choke each other out. Mix the seeds in the hopper before spreading. Apply one-half of the total amount of required seed in one direction and the second half at right angles to the first. Rake the area lightly to barely cover the seeds with soil.

If you have access to a roller, roll the seedbed to guarantee that all seed comes in contact with the soil. Water gently but deeply. Continue to water every day (or whenever the soil looks dry) until 3 weeks after the seeds germinate. To prevent seeds from washing away, water slowly to keep the soil evenly moist. When the grass is 2 to 2½ inches tall, mow it to a height of 1½ to 2 inches; mow regularly thereafter.

1 If the existing soil is poor, add 4 to 6 inches of topsoil or sphagnum peat moss. Cultivate with a rotary tiller or spade to a depth of 4 inches.

2 After removing any stones, twigs, or other debris, rake the surface as level as possible. If liming is necessary, incorporate the lime into the soil prior to leveling.

Sod (*above*) will give you an instant lawn. Unlike seeds, sod will establish itself fast and with little competition from weeds. Bluegrass sod is the best because it quickly weaves a close-knit, vigorous, and attractive turf.

When you choose sod, look for well-rooted, moist rolls that are uniformly green and not yellowing. After you get the sod home, install it as soon as possible, especially during very hot weather; don't let more than 2 to 3 days go by, even in cool weather. Store the sod in a cool, shaded area and moisten it if it starts to dry out before being laid.

Prepare the soil as you would for seeding. The soil under the sod should be moistened before it's laid, and the lawn should be kept watered for several weeks until the grass is established. Sodding can be done even in the summer, provided you keep the sod moist.

3 Apply lawn fertilizer at the rate of 2 pounds of nitrogen per 1,000 square feet. For even distribution, use a clean drop spreader.

4 After these tasks are completed, water the area thoroughly with a gentle spray from a garden hose to allow the soil to settle.

Some grasses, such as zoysia, bermuda grass, and St. Augustine, are sold as plugs (small sections of sod) or sprigs (pieces of stem taken from sod). Plant these in early spring, up to 12 inches apart; keep moist before planting.

CARE AND MAINTENANCE

Your lawn will need a little extra help if you want it to wear well and look its best. Follow these tips for a healthy turf.

WATERING
■ Water requirements for lawns vary depending on soil, rainfall, and type of grass. A lawn with sandy soil will need to be watered more often than one with clay soil. Some cool-climate grasses, like bluegrass, will need more water than drought-tolerant types, such as fescue.

Your lawn will show these signs when it's dry and needs water: (1) grass turns from a rich green to a bluish cast; (2) turf loses resiliency so footprints remain longer; and (3) growth is substantially slowed. To encourage deep roots, water to a depth of at least 6 inches.

FERTILIZING
■ A fertilizer rich in nitrogen, phosphorus, and potassium will help keep your lawn looking lush. In the spring, apply a fertilizer with a nutrient ratio of 2-1-1. For most lawns, 1 pound of nitrogen per 1,000 square feet is plenty. Feed again in the fall, in the ratio of 1-2-2, to encourage healthy root growth before the ground freezes. Nitrogen applied before winter should be the water-insoluble, slow-release kind.

THATCH REMOVAL
■ A small amount of thatch—an accumulation of dead stems and roots—is beneficial to a lawn because it becomes an organic fertilizer as it breaks down. A heavy buildup of thatch, however, prevents penetration of moisture and nutrients into the soil and may harbor insects and disease. To keep thatch at a healthy level, remove excess material once a year with a power rake.

Don't let leaves or other objects (such as lawn furniture and toys) remain on the lawn for any longer than necessary, or the grass under them will quickly lose color.

For even distribution, apply fertilizer with a spreader instead of by hand. To avoid lines, apply half of the fertilizer in one direction and the other half at right angles.

If you're cutting an area out of the lawn for a new flower bed or patio, you may want to save the sod and relocate it to a sparse area. To lift the sod, place a flat spade under the roots, cut, and roll.

Repairing bare spots is like starting a new lawn. Remove dead grass, improve the soil, fertilize, lime if needed, seed or sod, and water regularly. Avoid walking on the new grass until it's established.

LAWN WEEDS

Name	Comments	Controls
Chickweed, Mouse-Ear *Cerastium*	Creeping perennial that forms dense matlike growth. Tiny white flowers appear from April into October. Prefers moist, cool conditions. Grows in most areas except along Mexican border or in North Dakota.	Difficult to pull, because it entangles in the grass. Control by applying a postemergent herbicide.
Crabgrass, Common *Digitaria sanguinalis*	An annual grass found across the country, except in the Southwest and southern Florida. Blooms July to October. Doesn't grow in shade—likes moisture and sun. Seeds mature in late summer and early fall.	Follow a good cultural schedule to choke out. Mow lawn high during spring to shade germinating seedlings. Apply a preemergent control in early spring.
Dandelion *Taraxacum officinale*	Found across the country except in a few areas of deep South. Produces coarse-toothed, long leaves in bunch and yellow blooms, followed by round white seed heads. In cold areas, flowers from March until frost.	The entire taproot must be dug out; otherwise, a new plant will grow. Use a postemergent herbicide in fall. Spot chemical applicators are available for use in spring and summer.
Dock, Curly *Rumex crispus*	A perennial with a 1½- to 2-foot taproot. Produces one or more tall stems. Found across the country. Its spikes of whitish flowers appear from June into September.	If infestation is small, dig it out, being sure to get the entire taproot. On larger area, apply a postemergent herbicide. Apply spray into each plant crown for best results.
Lamb's-Quarters *Chenopodium album*	Common annual weed. Leaves are gray-green on top and have white underside. Occurs most in newly seeded lawns or lawns with thin turf. Plumelike whitish flower heads and seeds appear from June to October.	Mow lawn closely. Soak soil for easy pulling. For large area, use postemergent herbicide.

Name	Comments	Controls
Plantain, Broad-Leaved *Plantago major*	A perennial (sometimes annual) with broad leaves, 3 to 6 inches long and bunched low to ground. Tall, slender stalks bear pencil-shape flowers from June to October. Found across the country. Spreads by seeds.	If infestation is small, dig it out when soil is moist. For a larger area, use a postemergent herbicide in the early spring or fall.
Quack Grass, or Couch Grass *Agropyron repens*	A hardy, vigorously spreading perennial bunchgrass. Forms a dense root structure by rooting at every joint on underground stems. Found across the country except in parts of the Southwest and deep South.	Cannot be eradicated without killing lawn grasses, too. A black plastic cover extended over a patch will starve all growth. Or apply a postemergent control; wait three weeks before reseeding lawn.
Shepherd's Purse *Capsella bursa-pastoris*	A persistent annual that forms a circle of low leaves with white flowers on tall stems. Seedpods are flat and heart-shape like a shepherd's purse.	Fairly easy to pull if soil is moist. Soak soil before pulling. For larger area, use a postemergent herbicide.
Thistle, Canada *Cirsium arvense*	Thrives in clay soils in the North. Long prickly leaves and lavender flowers. Spreads by seeds and underground roots. Blooms July through October.	Use knife to cut belowground and remove crown from roots. For larger infestation of this weed, apply a postemergent herbicide.
Yarrow, Common, or Milfoil *Achillea millefolium*	Creeping perennial with very finely divided, soft leaves and white cushiony blooms. Grows in most regions with poor soil, except in the Southwest. Spreads by seeds and underground stems.	Dig weed out as soon as it appears. For larger area, control by a couple of applications of postemergent herbicide during the growing season.

LAWN PESTS

Insect	Description and Trouble Signs	Controls
Armyworms	These pests are found in dense groupings, feeding on grass to make a somewhat circular area. The caterpillar is up to 1½ inches long with green, tan, or black stripes on its back. Causes damage from spring through late summer.	Keep lawn healthy by watering and feeding on a regular schedule. Apply a slow-release urea-formaldehyde lawn fertilizer. Control pest with Diazinon at first sign of extensive feeding.
Billbugs	Adults are ¼-to-¾-inch long, black or reddish-brown beetles with long snout. They chew holes in stems of grass, depositing eggs in them. Eggs hatch into chunky, legless, ½-inch-long larvae, which puncture stem and crown as they feed. They kill grass in patches; grass blades break off at soil line.	In lawns with a history of billbug damage, treat in the early spring with Diazinon or carbaryl to control adult beetles. Or, treat in the early summer to control larvae.
Chinch bugs	Adults have black bodies with white wings and reddish legs. Nymphs grow from very small size to ⅛-inch-long adults. They prefer dry, sunny areas. Chinch bugs feed at all stages of their development, leaving large yellowish-to-brown patches.	Well-fed lawns discourage this pest. Treat the two generations of this insect in June and August with Diazinon or carbaryl.
Cutworms	Smooth grayish or brownish caterpillars, up to 2 inches long; feed at night after hiding under protective covering during the day. They cut off grass at the soil line and can be a problem from spring until late summer. Cutworms eat away grass stems at soil surface, leaving small dead spots.	If affected area is small, it can be puddled with water to bring worms to the surface to collect and destroy. Control with carbaryl or Diazinon.
Grubs, White	Grubs are the larvae of beetles, including Japanese and June beetles. Larvae are thick, whitish, C-shape underground worms that vary from ¾ to 1½ inches in length. Grubs eat grass roots, leaving brown, dead patches easily lifted out of the lawn.	In small areas, cut away sections of sod; pick and destroy grubs from underside. In severe infestations, control with Diazinon.

Insect	Description and Trouble Signs	Controls
Leafhoppers	These yellow, brown, or green wedge-shape insects are less than ½ inch long. When you walk across a lawn, they flit away. They are especially active on East and West coasts, but can be found anywhere. They suck juices from leaves, causing grass to turn white, later yellow, then brown.	Control with Diazinon or carbaryl when leafhoppers are most abundant.
Mites	Clover mites show as tiny red specks against white paper. They are found in lawns across the country. Bermuda grass mites are pale green and microscopic; they may occur in Gulf Coast and western lawns. All spiderlike mites suck juices from grass leaves. Grass wilts, turns yellow, and dies.	Because overly succulent grass growth attracts mites, avoid heavy fertilization of your lawn. Control with Diazinon at first sign of infestation.
Mole crickets	These brownish insects are about 1½ inches long and mostly a problem in southern lawns. They cut off underground stems and roots in the day and work on stems at night, leaving lawns with areas that appear closely clipped. They like moist, warm weather.	Control with Diazinon.
Nematodes	Transparent roundworms with whitish or yellowish tint. They are tiny, often microscopic. Their presence may not be realized until a bleached-out area is apparent. The pests feed mainly on grass roots but some feed on stems and leaves. Disease may set in because of weakened turf.	To avoid and suppress nematodes, keep turf well fed and water on schedule. Won't require chemical treatment.
Sod webworms	These tan-colored moths, about ¾ inch long, lay eggs at dusk. Gray or light brown larvae up to 1 inch long feed on bluegrasses and bent grasses, doing most damage from spring to midsummer. Feed on shoots and crowns of grass, causing irregular, close-clipped brown patches.	Treat with carbaryl or Diazinon when larvae are present.

GROUND COVERS IN THE LANDSCAPE

Pachysandra (*right,* back) and ajuga (*right,* front) are two popular ground covers. They prosper in rich, moist soil in a shaded or partly sunny spot. Ajuga, or bugleweed, grows 4 to 6 inches tall and quickly forms a dense mat of green, bronze, or variegated foliage. Its flowers, which are usually blue (but also may be pink or white), appear in spring. Pachysandra is an evergreen plant that grows 6 to 8 inches high, with scalloped, shiny green leaves and tiny white blooms in the spring. Varieties also are available with green leaves edged in white.

Another good choice for moist, shaded areas is wintercreeper (*Euonymus fortunei*), which offers attractive foliage. It roots itself as it trails along the ground.

Deep shade won't hamper the spread of sweet woodruff (*Asperula odorata*). This delightful, low-growing ground cover (*right*) grows rapidly when tucked under and between trees and low shrubs. Only a few inches high, it produces delicate white flowers in spring over star-like leaves.

Good companion plants for sweet woodruff include one of the many hostas (back of photo, *right*), best known for their textured and variegated foliage; periwinkle (*Vinca minor*), which produce blue flowers in the spring; the hardy ivies, for their many leaf types and forms; silver-edged lamium, useful in problem spots; epimedium, which have heart-shaped leaves that hide tiny pink or yellow flowers; and ferns.

Shrublike ground covers, such as the heaths and heathers at *left*, offer soft textures and subtle colors with evergreen needles and pink, white, or red blossoms. Although heath (erica) blooms in spring and heather (calluna) blooms in the fall, both have similar care requirements. They need full sun to produce flowers, and an acidic, moist, very poor soil to thrive. Clip when overgrown and mulch well for winter.

Low-growing shrubs also make excellent ground covers. At the top of the list are cotoneasters, which bear tiny white flowers and bright berries. Other good shrub candidates include ground-hugging junipers, honeysuckle, jasmine, hypericum, broom, sarcococca, skimmia, bearberry, and holly.

When environmental factors such as heat, moisture, or soil pH limit your shrub choices, select a native ground cover that is better suited to your conditions. When you pick plants indigenous to your climate, they will grow better and you'll have less care. The California hillside pictured at *left* is planted with cacti, succulents, ice plant, pepper tree, statice, and palms—a perfect example of a nontraditional use of ground covers. Sedums and live-forevers also thrive in hot, dry spots.

If moist soils prevail, try bog andromeda, forget-me-not, or watercress (if you have running water nearby). Salty sea breezes won't bother thrift, pine, lamb's-ears, bearberry, and some ornamental grasses.

GALLERY OF GROUND COVERS

Aegopodium podagraria
Bishop's weed or goutweed

This ground cover grows 8 to 10 inches tall, with a profusion of green and white variegated leaves and a cluster of white flowers. It will thrive under almost any condition. However, it tends to be weedy and should be planted where the roots will be contained.

Ajuga reptans
Carpet bugle or bugleweed

Ajuga is happy in sun or shade and prefers a moist soil. Blue flower spikes rise 4 to 6 inches high over the foliage in mid-spring; rosettes of shiny green or bronze leaves lie flat on the ground. Ajuga is useful in self-contained borders around patios or front entrances.

BUTTERCUP
Ranunculus species

Buttercup covers a variety of plants, from those that are decorative to others that are more weedy. The flowers are yellow or white, appearing in mid-May over leaves and stems that creep along the ground. Some members of this family adapt well to rock gardens.

IVY
English ivy: *Hedera helix*
Boston ivy: *Parthenocissus tricuspidata*

Ivy grows rapidly over the ground, as well as on walls and fences. It is tolerant of shade and poor soil, but will thrive in a rich, moist soil. Boston ivy turns scarlet in the fall.

Lamium species
Dead nettle

Like other members of the mint family, lamium grows rapidly to fill in empty spaces. Leaves are silver and green; flowers are purple or yellow in spring. Lamium prefers partial shade and tends to get weedy.

LIRIOPE
Lilyturf

Evergreen in warm areas, liriope has grasslike leaves that are green or variegated and spikes of lilac-blue or white flowers that appear in fall. This tufted ground cover will grow equally well in sun or shade. Propagate by division.

EPIMEDIUM
Epimedium grandiflorum

This plant has wiry stems with heart-shape leaves that turn from light green to red in fall. Spring blooms are yellow or pink, forming underneath the foliage. Epimedium likes sun or partial shade. It is well suited to rock gardens, and will grow under trees.

Euonymus fortunei
Wintercreeper

This ground cover belongs to a large family of shrubs and vines. Evergreen plants vary in color from green to purple. Rooting as it trails along, winter creeper is good on banks for erosion control. Use in full sun or light shade.

FERNS
Variety of genera and species

Grown from spores rather than seeds, ferns are best loved for their performance in deep shade and cool, woodland areas. An organic soil kept moist is best. Watch for delicate fronds that emerge from the ground in spring.

ORNAMENTAL GRASS
Variety of genera and species

Ornamental grasses are especially good for use in full sun or for slopes and dry, sandy locations. Tall plumes of pampas grass, graceful arches of fountain grass, or blue festucas add interest and color to any landscape.

Pachysandra terminalis
Japanese spurge

This plant is one of the most popular selections for carpeting the ground in a moist, shady area. Dark, evergreen leaves, 6 to 8 inches tall, are topped in the spring with small, white flowers. Spreads slowly, but worth waiting for.

Vinca minor
Periwinkle, creeping myrtle

Dark, shiny leaves are topped by a multitude of lavender flowers in mid-spring. An evergreen growing in sun in zones 4 to 7, or shade in all areas, vinca grows well in all but the poorest soil. Good for slopes. Vinca divides easily.

CHOOSING AND USING GROUND COVERS

Ground covers play a vital role in landscape design—it's hard to picture a perfect landscape without them. But when you plan your ground covers, you need to consider more than appearance. You must be sure you're choosing the right plant for the right spot, considering light, climate, moisture, soil, and use.

LANDSCAPE USES
■ Traditionally, ground covers are used to form a carpet under and between trees and shrubs where grasses have difficulty growing. Along with being aesthetically pleasing, ground covers also reduce weeds and conserve soil moisture for the trees and shrubs around them. Where only a few shrubs or trees appear in a simple landscape design, a complementary ground cover will tie the plants into a unit, serving as a base or a platform.

Ground covers are also good solutions for slopes or other spots where grasses will not grow, or would be difficult to maintain. A ground cover will add color and interest to these otherwise bare settings, and prevent erosion on steep grades. When you choose a ground cover for a hillside, select one with a heavy root system that will knit in with the soil. Good choices include ivy, hosta, daylilies, or ice plant.

Very low-growing plants, such as thrift, pearlwort, creeping thyme, sedum, and baby's-tears, work well as fillers between stepping-stones. These plants make a soft cushion that is aromatic when stepped on. You also can use ground covers to direct traffic away from an area. Or plant them in crevices of retaining walls to add color.

If pachysandra (*above*) is not held in bounds, it may encroach upon a lawn or path. Use brick or metal edgings to restrain growth.

SPECIAL FEATURES
■ Faced with a spot where nothing will grow? Many ground covers stand up to the most adverse growing conditions. Those types that tolerate poor soil and dry locations, for example, include foamflower, lamium, goutweed, crown vetch, and sedum. Where rocks and outcroppings create awkward-to-plant nooks and crags, you can fill in with rock cress, thrift, candytuft, Irish moss, pearlwort, and santolina.

Consider foliage in choosing ground covers. Many have unusual colors and add lovely highlights. Ground covers with bright foliage include bronze ajuga, blue festuca, silver snow-in-summer, or purple wintercreeper. Flowers, too, add needed color to the landscape design, from spring's gold alyssum and white candytuft to fall's purple liriope.

At least once a year (more often if necessary), trim euonymus (*above*) to encourage thicker growth and make a neater appearance.

When you need a ground cover in a spot near an open window or next to a deck, choose a fragrant plant such as lily-of-the-valley. Or for a double-duty cover-up, carpet your ground with an edible delight such as strawberries.

POST-PLANTING CARE
■ Whatever ground covers you select, they'll stay at their best if you follow a few basic maintenance steps. Plant ground covers in spring or fall and water until plants get established. Many drought-resistant varieties can go without watering, but even they do best when adequately watered. To prevent soil erosion, slowly apply water to slopes. Feed ground covers in early spring with a complete fertilizer, and mulch semihardy types in the fall in cold-winter areas.

1 When ground covers, such as the lamium *above,* become overcrowded, divide them and plant them elsewhere in your garden or share them with friends. Water well before lifting and pulling plants apart. Some tearing of roots is inevitable when you pull up the plants, but you can keep it to a minimum if you're careful.

Divide and replant ground covers in spring or fall. In the fall, leave enough time for roots to become established before the ground freezes. Plant ground covers at the same level they were growing before. Spacing depends on how quickly the plant grows and on your budget. If you set plants 6 inches apart, 100 plants will cover 25 square feet.

2 Lamium, a fast-growing cover plant, can be spaced farther apart than slow-growing types such as pachysandra and epimedium. Keep the area weed-free while plants are filling in.

3 Water well after planting until roots show new growth. Mulch to protect over the winter and to retain moisture in the spring. Obtain new plants from nurseries or mail-order catalogs.

VINES IN THE LANDSCAPE

Vines offer inexpensive, practical solutions for hard-to-solve landscape problems in a yard. A large flowering vine like wisteria can be used to soften the sharp architectural lines of an exposed porch, deck, or patio. And, at the same time, the plant will add shade, privacy, and beauty to the setting. Smaller vines, such as clematis and plumbago, will easily disguise a porch pillar, stairway railing, arbor, or small shed. If you need to camouflage a fence or wall, vines like Dutchman's pipe, trumpet vine, star jasmine, and honeysuckle are hard to beat.

Place evergreen vines on the north side of your house, and deciduous vines on the south or west side. Evergreen types will insulate walls year-round; deciduous types will provide shade in the summer and let the sun into the house during the winter.

When you select a vine, consider its growth rate versus your available space. Consider also bloom time, color, fragrance, and foliage texture. Some vines will cling directly to the house; others need to be grown on a sturdy support, such as a trellis, arbor, or fence.

Use clematis (*above*) to perk up a wall with show-stopping blooms in May and June. Unlike many other vines, clematis is easy to control, rarely growing over 12 feet long.

The delicate fragrance and pastel blooms of the wisteria (*above*) have made it a favorite with gardeners across the country. A good choice for a porch or overhead structure, wisteria produces long clusters of blue, rose, or white flowers in May. Useful in the same way in warm climates is the exotic and bright bougainvillea (*opposite*). This vine looks terrific when trained around doors and windows.

A fence can be turned into a backdrop of green with a vine like honeysuckle (*above*). Without support, this versatile vine will carpet the ground to prevent erosion on steep slopes.

GALLERY OF ANNUAL AND PERENNIAL VINES

BLACK-EYED SUSAN VINE
Thunbergia alata

An annual, slow-growing vine bearing yellow, white, or orange flowers with a dark throat. Grows in sun or shade but likes moist soil. Try it as a ground cover or in hanging baskets. Black-eyed susan does best in hot areas.

CLEMATIS
Clematis species and varieties

This perennial boasts tiny to large blooms of white, blue, purple, yellow, or red, and is perfect on a fence, trellis, or pole. Give it some shade and an alkaline soil. Flowers have large, colorful spears instead of petals.

CLEMATIS, Autumn
Clematis paniculata

One of the hardiest of the clematis, the fall or sweet autumn clematis is filled with many fragrant white blooms in late summer and early fall. An outstanding display of berries follows the flowering season.

MORNING-GLORY
Ipomoea alba

Morning-glory has flowers in white, blue, purple, red, or pink that open in the morning and close by the afternoon. This annual grows rapidly and prefers sun and poor soil. Use as a screen; don't let it get weedy.

PLUMBAGO
Plumbago auriculata

Actually a shrubby climber, plumbago is hardy only in warm climates. The pale blue flowers that are less than one inch across bloom all summer. It prefers full sun but tolerates dry soil and drought conditions.

PORCELAIN VINE
Ampelopsis brevipedunculata

This perennial vine has lovely, pea-size berries that are clustered and change from a pale lavender in spring to yellow in fall to porcelain blue in winter. The plant grows fast and is covered with deeply lobed leaves.

CUP-AND-SAUCER VINE
Cobaea scandens

Perennial in the South and an annual in the north, this vine grows and attaches itself easily to supports. Hanging flowers produced on pendulous, 12-inch stems are lavender to purple. Blooms for 6 months for continuous color.

DUTCHMAN'S PIPE
Aristolochia durior

This perennial vine is quite hardy and vigorous, with small white or purple flowers, shaped like a pipe. Leaves are large, round, and coarse, making the vine excellent for screening. A rapid grower good for covering buildings.

HYDRANGEA, climbing
Hydrangea anomala petiolaris

One of the best perennial vines, the climbing hydrangea has large clusters of small white flowers in early summer. It clings by rootlets. Prefers sun, but light shade is fine. Prune severely in autumn or early spring.

SILVER LACE VINE
Polygonum auberti

This perennial blooms in late summer and early fall when color is needed in the garden. A rapid-growing, dense plant with fragrant white flowers, especially good on fences. Full sun is best; dry soil is no problem.

STEPHANOTIS
Stephanotis floribunda

A perennial only in the warmest of locations and a popular greenhouse plant, stephanotis has tubular flowers of white or near white that appear during the summer. Leaves are long and abruptly pointed at the apex.

WISTERIA
Wisteria floribunda or *W. sinensis*

A popular perennial with a large number of spectacular clusters of blue, purple, or white flowers. It does best in sun and light soil kept moist. The fragrance is outstanding. Wisteria does not transplant well.

CARE AND MAINTENANCE

Annual and perennial vines have different care requirements. Read below for some general maintenance tips.

ANNUAL VINES
■ Annual vines grow quickly, then die at the end of the season. Because they are lightweight, annual vines do not require heavy-duty supports. They rarely need pruning. You can purchase nursery-started plants, but most annual vines also can be grown from seed. Whether you start seeds indoors or out depends on how long they take to mature. If the vine matures quickly, sow seeds directly into the ground after danger of frost is past.

PERENNIAL VINES
■ Perennial vines will reward you year after year with blooms or lush foliage. Because perennial types eventually become woody and heavy, support them with a sturdy structure.

To keep growth controlled and attractive, prune perennial types annually. In early spring, remove all the dead wood. Nonflowering vines can be pruned at any time. For flowering vines, prune in early spring if they flower on new wood (this year's growth); prune after flowering if they bloom on old wood (last year's growth).

Vines used as ground covers may encroach upon the lawn, path, or other plantings unless they're kept in check. A metal or brick barrier may help, or you may need to trim them frequently.

Perennial vines are sold in pots, but you can also propagate an established plant by taking cuttings just below leaf axils. Place cuttings in sphagnum peat moss and perlite or vermiculite and cover with a plastic bag until rooted.

The vigorous, sun-loving trumpet vine (*above*) will dazzle you with clusters of colorful reddish-orange flowers from midsummer till frost. Plants cling to any surface, transforming it into a fountain of vivid color. Newer crimson- or yellow-flowering varieties are now available. Because this perennial vine spreads by underground runners, locate it where roots will be contained.

Vines grow and attach themselves to whatever is nearby. Some, such as the clematis, have twining stems that wrap around anything that will hold them upright.

The passionflower is supported by tendrils. Keep these vigorous, wandering vines away from any objects that you don't want them to cling to.

Ivy, trumpet vine, and winter-creeper send out rootlike holdfasts. Because they can pull off siding, use only on stone, brick, or concrete walls.

Vines without holdfasts may be difficult to attach to flat walls. For these types, insert a masonry hook into the mortar and guide the stem through it to train the vine to grow upright or into a pattern.

Twining vines or those with tendrils do well on trellises, arbors, or pergolas because they attach themselves quite readily. Other young vines can be run through the opening in latticework.

Some vines have difficulty clinging at all. To keep them vertical or growing where you want them, tie them to a support. Use a twist tie or a strip of loose fabric to prevent damaging the stem.

WILDFLOWERS

Tough landscaping problems in your yard will knuckle under to native plants and wildflowers. These sturdy, low-maintenance plants are debuting in gardens after growing wild in woodlands, prairies, and deserts, and along roadsides. Native plants and wildflowers naturally solve such challenges as steep slopes, densely shaded areas, low-lying wet spots, and dry hot places.

Study the natural conditions in your yard, including soil fertility, drainage, and the amount of sunlight or shade. Then match this information with the plants that are suited for your situation. Plants that are indigenous to your area will probably work best for you. Rather than remove plants from the wild, purchase seeds or plants from nurseries or mail-order catalogs.

The small woodland garden at *right* performs much like a natural forest. Such early-blooming wildflowers as jack-in-the-pulpit, marsh marigold, trillium, and bloodroot are followed by an equally brilliant summer show of royal fern, bluet, mayapple, bleeding-heart, Virginia bluebell, and wild geranium. True to nature's woodlands, these native gems are happier when left completely undisturbed.

Meadow flowers can be the ticket you need if you have a large sunny area in your yard that you'd rather not mow. Many seed companies are now offering native seed mixes, packaged for specific regions. Although plants spread quickly, brighter rewards will show up the second year. Each year, a different combination of plants will bloom.

WILDFLOWERS FOR SUN

- Aster, wild
- Black-eyed susan
- Blanketflower
- Blue gentian
- Blue lobelia
- Butterfly weed
- California poppy
- Evening primrose
- Forget-me-not
- Liatris
- Marsh marigold
- Purple coneflower
- Queen-Anne's-lace
- Rose mallow
- Sunflower
- Tickseed
- Virginia bluebells
- Yarrow

WILDFLOWERS FOR SHADE

- Bloodroot
- Cardinal flower
- Columbine
- Crested iris
- Dog-tooth violet
- Dutchman's-breeches
- Ferns
- Foamflower
- Jack-in-the-pulpit
- Jacob's-ladder
- Mayapple
- Partridgeberry
- Shooting-star
- Solomon's-seal
- Spiderwort
- Trillium
- Violet
- Wild ginger

GALLERY OF WILDFLOWERS

BLOODROOT
Sanguinaria canadensis

Related to the poppy, bloodroot has large, blue-green leaves and single flowers of pure white—sometimes tinged in pink—with a form similar to a water lily. Flowers open in the morning sunshine and close in the evening. The plant is so named because its roots, stems, and sap are blood red. Growing to about 10 inches in height, bloodroot brings a freshness to the mid-spring wildflower garden.

SOIL: Rich, acidic, moist, woodsy soil
LIGHT: Part or full shade
HARDINESS: Zone 4
COMMENTS: Bloodroot is one of the many wildflowers that thrive in deep woods and loves to grow through a covering of mulch. It can be grown from seeds or cuttings. If it is necessary to transplant, try to accomplish this by moving rhizomes in fall. Set in a spot where the roots will be cool.

COLUMBINE
Aquilegia canadensis

The plant looks fragile, but actually it's quite hardy, surviving cold winters and barren, rock-filled meadows. Growing 18 to 24 inches tall on thin stems, columbine sways easily in the breeze. Flowers come in any color or combination of colors, with interesting spurs that swing out behind the blooms and resemble a bird in flight. Leaves are medium-size and scalloped.

SOIL: Dry, sandy soil
LIGHT: Part shade
HARDINESS: Zone 3
COMMENTS: If your late spring or early summer garden could use a sea of interesting, colored blooms, the columbine is the answer. Columbine plants are easy to grow from divisions or from seeds; often they are not long-lived, so it is best to start new plants every few years. Hummingbirds, bees, and other wildlife are attracted to the columbine.

COWSLIP (marsh marigold)
Caltha palustris

Golden yellow clusters of 2-inch, buttercuplike flowers bloom in the early spring on plants about 8 to 16 inches tall. Leaves are large and lush, and somewhat heart-shape. These plants are bog or marsh plants—as the name implies—and must be in wet soil at all times. Therefore, plant them at the side of ponds, rivers, streams, or any other wet area. Combine them with water iris, bog andromeda, or watercress.

SOIL: Wet, marshy, slightly acidic soil
LIGHT: Full sun or light shade
HARDINESS: Zone 4
COMMENTS: Cowslip will die to the ground after blooming, and will do fine the following year if the soil dries out a bit over the summer. Easy to grow, cowslip can be propagated from root divisions or seeds. The flower buds can also be cooked and eaten, and in that way resemble capers.

DUTCHMAN'S-BREECHES
Dicentra cucullaria

This close relative of the bleeding-heart has finely cut, lacy foliage similar to that on the bleeding-heart. The flowers are white, with a yellow trim that looks like old-fashioned breeches hanging upside down to dry on a clothesline. A typical plant is no more than 12 inches tall, with flowers appearing just above the foliage in mid-spring.

SOIL: Rich, slightly alkaline soil
LIGHT: Moderate to heavy shade
HARDINESS: Zone 3
COMMENTS: As the foliage dies down and disappears after blooming, be prepared to fill in with shady annuals if necessary. Dutchman's-breeches like the woods, shaded streams, and rocky areas. These plants grow from corms, like to have good drainage, and can be increased by offsets from the corms, root divisions, or seeds.

GINGER, WILD
Asarum canadense

Six-inch-wide, slightly ruffled and hairy leaves produce a single, small, brownish-purple flower at the junction of the leaf stem. The three-lobed flower can be difficult to spot. The wild ginger is sometimes called the monkey jug plant because the open flower resembles a little brown jug. Blooms appear in mid-spring at the base of 4- to 6-inch plants.

SOIL: Very rich, moist, slightly acidic soil is best for these plants.
LIGHT: Part to heavy shade
HARDINESS: Zone 3
COMMENTS: Used as a naturalized addition to the garden or as a ground cover, wild ginger has a creeping rootstalk that spreads along ground areas. In the past, the roots of wild ginger were used as a substitute for ginger in preparing recipes. Propagate wild ginger by root divisions or seeds.

HEPATICA (liverleaf)
Hepatica americana

In cold areas, hepatica may bloom before the snow melts. This woodland plant has single, ¾-inch blooms of lavender, blue, white, or pink before the foliage pops up. The leaves are three-lobed, very soft, and furry when young, thickening as they mature. Flower stems are also hairy and only 4 to 6 inches tall. The hepatica is found in wooded areas and is a good choice for naturalized spots in your garden.

SOIL: Rich, moist, well-drained, slightly acidic soil
LIGHT: Heavy shade
HARDINESS: Zone 4
COMMENTS: These flowers look like blue or pink buttercups with white centers. Place them where you can admire them, as they are small and could otherwise be easily missed.

GALLERY OF WILDFLOWERS

JACK-IN-THE-PULPIT
Arisaema triphyllum

This wildflower is grown for its unusual blooms that appear in late spring. These flowers form under two stems with large, three-parted leaves, each part being 2 to 3 inches long. Plants produce one flower per stem; the long, tubular-shaped, green and purple striped spathe grows up and over the central spike, or spadix, similar to a canopy or hood. A cluster of red berries, dazzling in color, appears in late fall. Ultimate plant height reaches 12 to 18 inches.

SOIL: Rich, well-drained, moist soil
LIGHT: Part shade
HARDINESS: Zone 4
COMMENTS: The Indians knew that this plant's roots, when cooked, are edible, hence, the plant's other common name, Indian turnip. Set jack-in-the-pulpit deeply at planting time, because roots grow very large. Propagate by seeds or root offshoots for best results.

MAYAPPLE
Podophyllum peltatum

Large colonies of mayapples—up to 100 or more—will fill in shady wooded gardens quickly. The leaves form a thick covering above the woodland floor with two types of foliage. Both are heavily lobed. One grows singly; the other grows in a pair. A white, apple-like blossom with a yellow center rises from a fork in the stem in April and May. The lovely 1- to 2-inch, six-petaled bloom nods to its surroundings. A yellow fruit called the mayapple follows in late summer. Although they look edible, mayapples are poisonous.

SOIL: Rich, moist soil
LIGHT: Part or full shade
HARDINESS: Zone 3
COMMENTS: Mayapples spread quickly by underground stolons, reaching a height of 2 feet to make a compact ground cover.

PHLOX, WOODLAND
Wild blue phlox (*Phlox divaricata*)

Also called sweet william, the woodland phlox is a wild cousin of the popular garden phlox. Its sky-blue blossoms grow in loose clusters on top of single stalks. A typical flat flower grows up to 1½ inches across. Blooms are light blue to lavender in color. Plants reach up to 12 inches in height, blooming in late spring through early summer. A prostrate form, called the creeping phlox, makes an excellent ground cover.

SOIL: Good, deep, slightly acidic soil
LIGHT: Open shade or dappled sun
HARDINESS: Zone 3
COMMENTS: This plant does well in a moist, open woodland setting, in a rock garden, or as an over planting for bulbs. Flowers have a slight fragrance. Plants grow easily and quickly from cuttings, divisions, or seeds. Transplant in either spring or fall.

SPRING-BEAUTY
Claytonia virginica

Buds nod and open into snappy, up-right flowers of pale pink with a darker pink veining, a white eye, and yellow stamens. Blooms are single, with five petals, formed in a loose cluster. Eight to ten flowers are borne on each stem, which grows from the base of the foliage. Leaves are narrow and grasslike. Bloom time is early spring; plant height varies from 6 to 10 inches.

SOIL: Spring-beauty will tolerate a variety of soils, but does best in a very moist, rich, woodsy soil.

LIGHT: Part shade

HARDINESS: Zone 7

COMMENTS: This is one of the loveliest ground covers for the spring garden. Spring-beauty grows from bulbous roots and is propagated from seed or divisions in spring or fall. However, it often will self-sow.

TRILLIUM (wake-robin)
Trillium grandiflorum

Another plant from the rich woods that grows in large colonies, spreading by rhizomes that are deep growing, thick, and fleshy. Three-petaled flowers grow one to a stem, nodding slightly. Starting off white, they turn soft pink as they age. The flower forms atop a fleshy stem above a trio of sharply pointed, 2- to 6-inch leaves. The plant grows 8 to 14 inches tall and blooms in early spring. Berries form when the plant is finished flowering.

SOIL: Good, rich, acidic soil

LIGHT: Prefers part shade, but sometimes does fine in the sun.

HARDINESS: Zone 5

COMMENTS: When transplanting trillium, dig deeply and don't disturb the roots. Propagate by seeds since it is almost impossible to divide the roots successfully. There is also a purple flowering trillium (*T. erectum*) which is similar, but unpleasant smelling.

VIOLET, DOG-TOOTH (trout lily)
Erythronium americanum

This dainty flower resembles a lily more than a violet. Six golden yellow, nodding petals are formed one to a stem. Long stamens hang from the center of the bloom. Thin stems grow from the center of two basal leaves, which are lance- or tongue-shape. Leaves, often mottled purple, make an interesting ground cover. Flowers reach 1 inch across; the plant grows to about 12 inches. After blooming in mid-spring, the plant goes dormant.

SOIL: Deep, moist, rich soil

LIGHT: Part to heavy shade

HARDINESS: Zone 4

COMMENTS: Treat dog-tooth violet, which actually grows from a corm, as you'd treat a bulb. Set 2 to 3 inches deep and 4 to 5 inches apart. You also can propagate from seeds. Plant in clumps in rock gardens or woodland gardens, or near streams.

SUMMER BULBS

Summer-blooming bulbs (which actually can be bulbs, tubers, rhizomes, roots, or corms) are less hardy than their springtime cousins. Because they are sensitive to freezing temperatures, such tender bulbs as caladium, dahlia, tuberous begonia, canna lily, calla lily, and gladiolus should be planted in the spring and dug up and stored each fall.

Fancy-leaved caladiums (*right*) are popular for their color-splashed, heart-shaped foliage. Serving double duty, these tender bulbs grow well either in the ground or in planters. Caladiums are bright performers in shady areas, but they're more vibrant when grown in partial sunlight. Choose among combinations of bright red, green, pink, silver, and white.

The exotic canna lily grows 6 feet tall, and produces attractive bronze or green foliage and large blossoms in red, orange, salmon, apricot, coral, pink, yellow, and white. New canna hybrids grow only about half as tall. Best used as accents, cannas need full sunlight.

Gladiolus make spectacular cut flowers. Their dramatic solid and two-toned flower spikes can be grown en masse in a special cutting garden, or in a mixed border with annuals and perennials. Gladiolus bloom 2 to 3 months after they're planted. Keep the garden in full flower by planting them in succession every two weeks. Glads fall over easily, so you may need to stake them. Use inconspicuous bamboo stakes tied with string to support the plants' stems and swordlike, vertical foliage.

SUMMER BULBS IN THE LANDSCAPE

Versatile and easy to care for, summer bulbs will fit anywhere in your garden. Careful planning at planting time will reward you with color all summer.

Dahlias offer an almost unlimited selection of heights, colors, and flower styles, and bloom willingly without being coddled. Their flowers cover the color spectrum, blooming in every shade but blue. Blossom types include single, peony, anemone, cactus, ball, and pompon. Tall, standard dahlias reach 6 feet or more and need staking. Newer dwarf varieties also are available that require no staking, making them ideal bedding plants. Dahlias are most often grown from tubers, but may also be started from seed.

Tuberous begonias flourish in shady areas. Different blossom shapes resemble a rose, camellia, or carnation. Available in both single and double forms, the blooms are up to 10 inches across, and come in white, pink, red, orange, yellow, or salmon; often, they are edged with a contrasting color.

Calla lilies, often grown as houseplants, also do well outdoors in partial shade. Their funnel-shaped pink, yellow, or white flowers bloom over handsome green or spotted foliage 8 weeks after they're planted.

Perfect for shady areas, tuberous begonias can be planted in pots (*above*) to brighten a drab corner on your deck or patio. Trailing types are tailor-made for hanging baskets. Plant tubers 1 inch deep in all-purpose potting soil.

Dahlias look striking in a bed of their own or scattered with annuals and perennials in a mixed flower border. The single-flowered types at *left* bloom with chrysanthemums in the fall when most other flower borders have little or no color.

Caladiums will grow as vigorously in containers as they do in the ground. On the shady patio *opposite*, their variegated foliage blends with potted marigolds and wax begonias to set a colorful stage for relaxing with a good book.

CARE AND MAINTENANCE

Like all bulbs, summer-flowering bulbs require a soil with excellent drainage. Before planting each spring, spade in organic matter as you prepare the soil (see *Soil*, page 4). Work the soil several inches deeper than the planting depth for the bulb.

STARTING BULBS INDOORS
■ While most summer bulbs can be planted directly outdoors in the spring, some types—including tuberous begonia, caladium, and calla lily—benefit from a 4- to 6-week head start indoors. For best results, plant the bulbs in a box or flat filled with an equal mixture of spaghnum peat moss and perlite. Set the box in a warm spot with bright indirect light. After all danger of frost is past, transplant the bulbs outdoors and water thoroughly.

WATERING
■ Water summer bulbs deeply and often. To prolong bloom time and keep disease to a minimum, avoid getting foliage and flowers wet. A mulch of organic material about 2 to 3 inches thick will help conserve moisture and keep roots cool when temperatures climb. All summer bulbs benefit from heavy feeding with a balanced fertilizer.

WINTER STORAGE
■ Because summer bulbs can't withstand cold temperatures, lift them from the ground each fall and store indoors in a dry, cool area over winter. Dig up tuberous begonias before the first expected fall frost. Other bulbs should remain in the ground until the foliage is blackened by frost. Be careful when digging not to cut or damage the roots, corms, tubers, or bulbs.

After digging up bulbs, wash off as much of the soil as possible with a gentle spray of water, and dry them in a sunny spot for several days. Follow these guidelines for storage:

Caladium: Place in a box or plastic bag of dry vermiculite, sphagnum peat moss, or sawdust; store at 60 degrees.

Canna: Dust with a fungicide and store, stem side down, at 45 to 50 degrees in any dry packing material.

Gladiolus: Store corms in mesh bags or old pantyhose, hung from the ceiling in a 35- to 40-degree room.

Dahlia: Allow to dry only slightly and store in a box or plastic bag filled with dry sphagnum peat moss or vermiculite at 35 to 40 degrees. Check bulbs frequently during the winter. If the roots start to shrivel, add a little water; if they start to grow (a sign that they're too

moist), open the container to let them dry out a little.

Tuberous begonia: Store in any dry packing material at 45 to 60 degrees.

Calla: Store in any dry packing material at 45 to 55 degrees.

Most other bulbs like a dry spot and a temperature around 50 to 60 degrees.

DIVIDING
■ If your summer bulbs need dividing, do it in spring just prior to planting. Cut roots and tubers with a sharp knife, making sure that each division contains at least one growing shoot or eye. True bulbs and corms produce offsets called bulblets or cormels, which can be pulled from the parent and planted separately. They may not bloom during their first year of growth, but in time they will mature to full size.

To produce large dahlia flowers, clip off side buds and allow only the center bud (*below*) to develop. This is known as "disbudding."

To produce compact, stockier dahlia plants with more flowers, pinch out the growing tip during the first 4 to 6 weeks.

Canna rhizomes should have at least two growing eyes. Lay them flat in the planting hole so the growing tip rests 1 inch below the soil line. Plant dwarf types 1 foot apart; standard types, 2 feet.

Plant dahlia tubers 4 inches deep, setting them flat in the planting hole. Tall dahlias need support. Drive a stake near the plant at planting time and tie the stem to the stake as it grows.

Gladiolus should be planted in clumps of four or more. Plant large corms 6 inches deep, and smaller ones 2 to 4 inches deep. Set stakes around the clump at planting time if stems need support.

1 Start tuberous begonias 4 to 6 weeks before the last expected frost. Plant the tubers, round side down, 1 inch deep, in potting soil. Overwatering will make tubers rot instead of sprout.

2 Grow in bright indirect light in a warm (65 degrees) spot. Move the pots outdoors when tops are about 3 inches tall and all danger of frost is past.

3 In summer, keep soil evenly moist; mist the foliage when the weather is very hot. Fertilize every week or two with a soluble plant food to produce an array of colorful blooms all season long.

CONSIDER YOUR CLIMATE

The climatic conditions in your area are a mixture of different weather patterns: sun, snow, rain, wind, and humidity. A good gardener is aware of all of the variations in temperature and conditions in his or her own garden, from how much rainfall it receives each year to the high and low temperatures of a typical growing season.

The zone map at *right* gives an approximate range of minimum temperatures across the country. Most plants are rated by these zones for conditions where they grow best.

However, zone boundary lines are not absolute. You can obtain the general information for your area from your state agricultural school or your county extension agent.

Be sure to study the microclimates that characterize your own plot of ground. Land on the south side of your house is bound to be warmer than a constantly shaded area exposed to cold, northwest winds. Being aware of the variations in your garden will help you choose the best plant for the prevailing conditions and avoid disappointment.

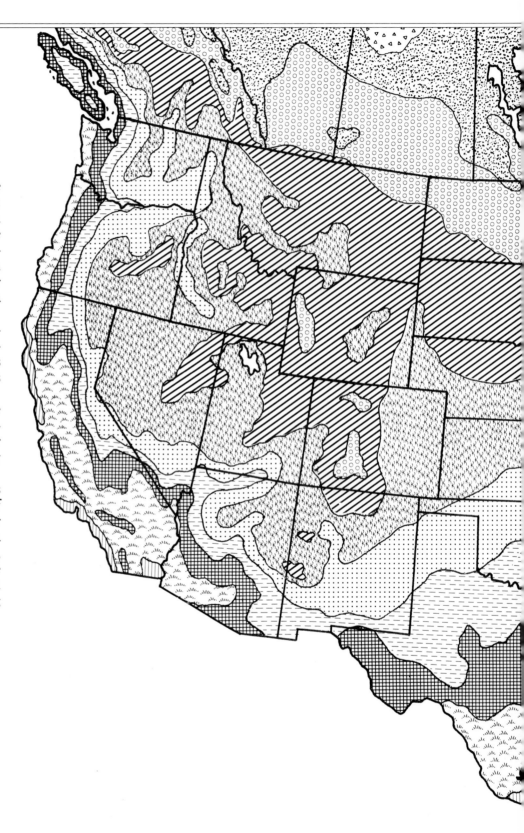

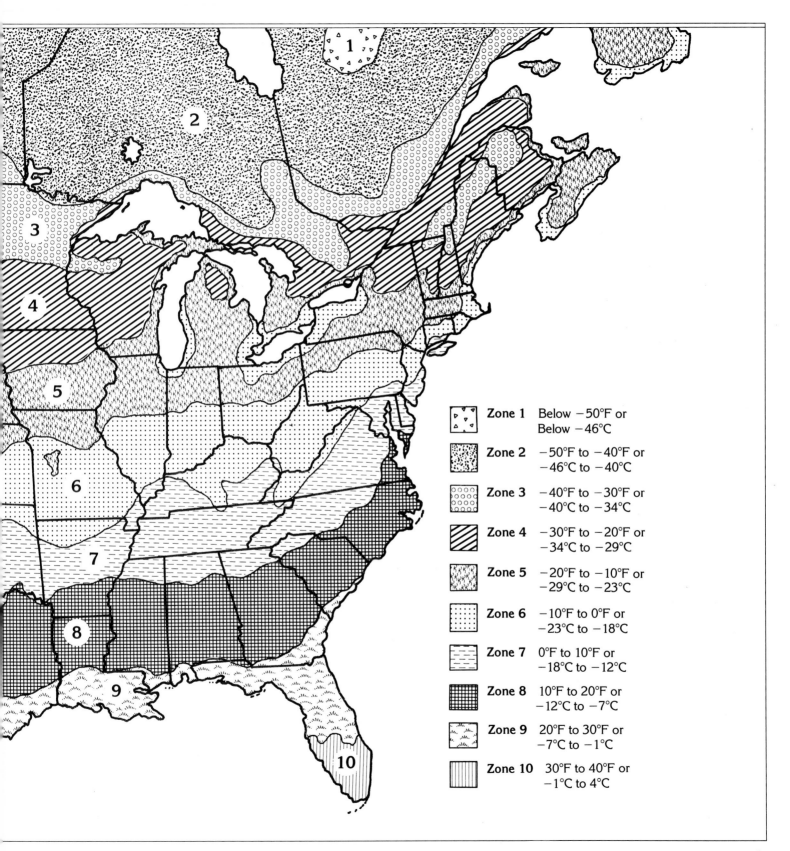

Zone 1 Below −50°F or Below −46°C

Zone 2 −50°F to −40°F or −46°C to −40°C

Zone 3 −40°F to −30°F or −40°C to −34°C

Zone 4 −30°F to −20°F or −34°C to −29°C

Zone 5 −20°F to −10°F or −29°C to −23°C

Zone 6 −10°F to 0°F or −23°C to −18°C

Zone 7 0°F to 10°F or −18°C to −12°C

Zone 8 10°F to 20°F or −12°C to −7°C

Zone 9 20°F to 30°F or −7°C to −1°C

Zone 10 30°F to 40°F or −1°C to 4°C

INDEX